Little Scientists
BIG Questions

Why Do Leaves Fall from Trees?

It's autumn!

Why do green leaves change colour in the autumn?

green

yellow

orange

red

brown

A tree's leafy story begins in **spring**.

The **Sun shines** and the days get **warmer**.

Drip Drip Drop

There are lots of rain showers, too.

The tree sucks up rainwater from the ground with its roots.

Little green buds shoot from its bare branches.

roots

bud

The tree is growing new green leaves.

Soon the tree's branches are covered with thousands of leaves.

The leaves have a very important job to do.

Just like you, a tree needs **food** so it can grow **bigger** and be **healthy.**

How does the tree get food?

The leaves make it!

9

Get ready for some BIG science!

A leaf needs **3** ingredients to make food.

1 Sunlight

2 Water

Water flows from a tree's roots, up its trunk, along its branches and into its leaves.

The water flows along these tiny veins.

Carbon dioxide

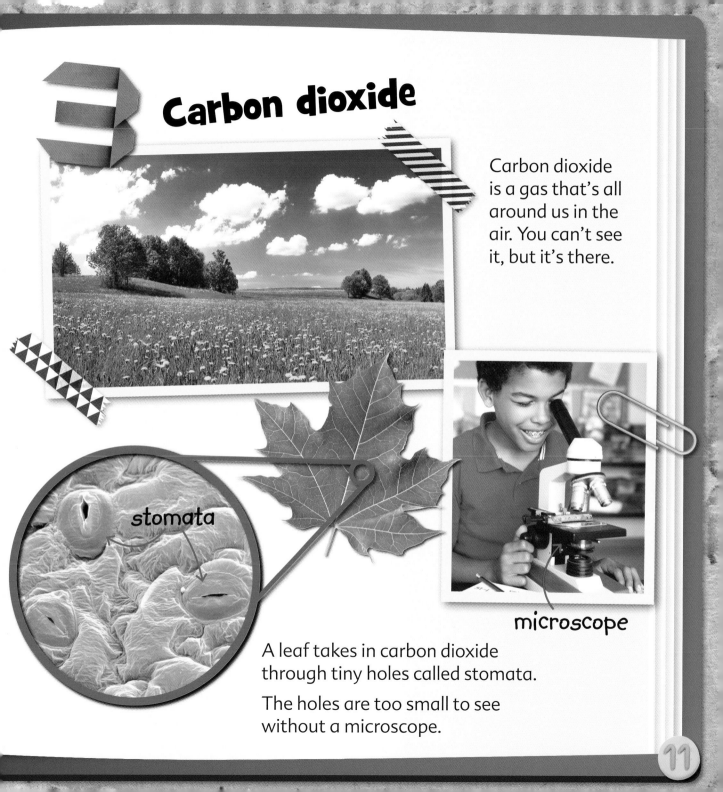

Carbon dioxide is a gas that's all around us in the air. You can't see it, but it's there.

stomata

microscope

A leaf takes in carbon dioxide through tiny holes called stomata.

The holes are too small to see without a microscope.

More BIG science coming up!

A leaf makes green stuff called chlorophyll.

**Let's say it!
"CHLOR-uh-fill"**

It's the chlorophyll that gives a leaf its green colour.

sunlight

The chlorophyll in a leaf traps sunlight.

It uses the sunlight to turn water and carbon dioxide into a sugary food for the tree.

water

carbon dioxide

As a leaf makes food, it also makes the oxygen that you breathe.

All **summer** the tree makes **food** inside its **leaves**.

When autumn comes, a tree must get ready for the tough months of winter.

Why is winter difficult for trees?

There is not enough sunlight for the leaves to make food.

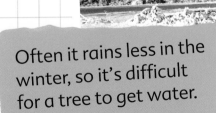

Often it rains less in the winter, so it's difficult for a tree to get water.

Water in the ground may freeze and become ice.

It's time for the tree to rest and save its energy.

The **tree** removes the **green** **chlorophyll** from its leaves.

Now its other **colours** can be seen.

These **colours** are normally **hidden**.

When spring comes, the tree will make chlorophyll again.

The leaves **stop** making **food.**

One by **one** they **die** and **drop** to the **ground.**

What happens to the dead leaves?

sssshhhhh

A hedgehog has made a cosy nest of leaves under the tree.

She goes to sleep until the spring.

Zzzzzzzzzzzzzzzz

18

Hundreds of **worms** live in the **soil** beneath the **tree**.

wood louse

We like to munch on dead leaves, too!

The **worms** like to eat dead **leaves**.

All through the winter
the tree rests.

But not all trees drop
their leaves and rest
in winter.

Evergreen trees drop some leaves and then regrow some all year round.

evergreen tree

These tough trees keep on making food, even in winter.

Some evergreen trees have long, thin leaves that look like needles.

Little **green buds** shoot from the tree's bare branches.

The tree is growing **new** green leaves to make food.

The tree's long winter rest is over.

Now we know why leaves fall from trees.
Good work, little scientists!

My Science Words

bud
A tiny new growth on a plant that becomes a flower or leaf.

carbon dioxide
An invisible gas in the air. As you breathe, you breathe out carbon dioxide.

chlorophyll
A green substance made by plants that they use for making food.

stomata
Tiny holes on a leaf that open and close, a little like tiny mouths.